A nest blew down

A nest blew down

Poems by

Casey Killingsworth

Cover design by Shay Culligan

ISBN: 978-1-954353-85-5

Kelsay Books
502 South 1040 East, A-119
American Fork, Utah, 84003

To some girl in a Catholic school uniform who doesn't remember my name. Thanks.

Acknowledgments

3rd Wednesday: "Obituarians dream in happy words"

A Handbook for Water: "A handbook for water"

Bath Magg: "Bad luck comes in threes"

Blue Moon: "Circus," "Building a legend out of Legos"

Bluepepper: "The first"

Cholla Needles: "To the next dove that comes around here"

COG: "Two friends in Bend," "Life coaches," "The guy who couldn't see color"

Down in the Dirt: "Natural selection poem," "Mars," "Manifold Destiny"

Galway Review: "Crow spreads his wings"

Gyroscope Review: "Zero in the denominator"

Hamline Lit: "Cub scout blows it with Catholic school girl"

Kimera: "If I were to define religion"

Open Arts Forum: "Thick as thieves," "Old maid"

Poetry Pacific: "Multiple choice"

Prometheus Dreaming: "Home run"

Star 82: "Reprise"

The American Journal of Poetry: "A nest blew down," "Nature/commerce," "What we can't afford to tell second graders"

The Pangolin Review: "The trophy case"

Two Thirds North: "Circus"

vox poetica: "My life as money"

Wilderness House: "Or so it seems to me"

Willawaw: "What if your job"

Contents

Circus

I saw on a television show once
that in the circus everyone has
two jobs. One is the glory job,
flying on the trapeze, knife
throwing, that sort of thing.
The other is the shirtsleeve job,
the everyday work, the cleaning up
elephant shit, the whatever.
The circus can't run unless
everyone does two jobs.

In my dreams my glory job is
to drive the train, the circus train,
pulling animals and clowns
around the world to smiling kids.
When I worked on the railroad all
we wanted was to be train drivers
instead of ground pukes
pushing ties under a thousand-pound rail,
all to keep some soft engineer riding
high on the way to some exotic place.

In my dreams my shirtsleeve job would
not be to stack cans on shelves all night in
a grocery store, would not be to
get held up at knifepoint one night
after the store is closed and we're locked in
waiting for the day shift puffs to let us out,
would not be to let a car run me over
on my bike my second night of work,
but still work my shift because
I'm too scared I'll get fired if I don't.

I would rather shovel elephant shit
than work in a grocery store
all night. But we all have to have two jobs,
we all have to live between the glory job
twirling on that trapeze, and
our shirtsleeve job, where safety
nets stretch every direction but never
stretch far enough to break our fall.

A nest blew down

It's not like losing a child
where you just sit there
and the child just sits there
but you're the only one
doing the talking.
It's more like a placenta
out of sticks and mud
in the driveway,
a former home where
something was born
and left, or maybe was
born and never got to
leave or was swept
away by the wind
that came through
here last night, maybe
more like having a house
burn to the ground,
no big deal if you have
wings to take you
somewhere else.

Reprise

Yesterday something delivered a short vision of what I thought the world was like thirty years ago; it hit me like that pain in your side the doctor said was nothing.

For two days now there's been a fisherman in the middle of the river, standing like an island there on such a day like today with all the rain and sad skies.

I wouldn't think there would be any fish in the river right now anyway but there he is, aiming his pole precisely toward a hole in the water

as if there were a guaranteed return if only he could hit that hole. I used to like fishing myself, not that I ever did it, but I liked watching the geometry of the line just before it hit the water,

waiting for the dumb fish to commit to swallowing the fake thrashing bug. I used to think fishing must be something good, a place you could bring your kids,

a memory you could casually fold in your pocket and discover years later when you pull that old pair of pants out of the closet and stuff your hands inside searching for forgotten prizes.

Now it's just one more hollow challenge, something you do because you told yourself you would, you'd get up this morning, you'd get up and wade knee-deep in some river, no matter what.

Two friends in Bend

For whatever reason my two childhood
friends ended up in Bend, a place

I have never lived. One just retired
from being some bigshot in some

big company and the other is there
because that's where they place people

who no longer remember their own names.
Sometimes I go and visit them,

the one to remember the old times,
and the other to remember the old times.

Bad luck comes in threes

I wrote something for my daughter, you know,
the one who's not here, because
that's what you're supposed to do. I guess.

Anyway about that same time I got held up
in the back of a store late one night, you know, the
bad-luck-comes-in-threes thing, and it was funny

that after it was all over the other store workers
were more scared than I was, looking over
their shoulders worrying about

whatever they couldn't see. The thing is
those workers never even saw the bad guys,
so maybe what scares us the most is

the unknown, even more than knife blades coming
for our skin, even more than trying to find out
where a daughter, who you had so looked forward to,

where did she go. To ease my pain someone
told me that the moment coming up, the one
that can still go either way, is the moment that counts.

What I'm trying to say here is my third piece
of bad luck was figuring out that waiting for
the next moment is supposed to be a good thing,

not whatever is really coming next,
but the uncertainty of it, you know,
because maybe it could have been some good luck.

Fan

To get the most out of your fan,
on the morning of a hot summer day
get up early and open all the windows
and shove the fan in front of one
of them and watch it seize
the cool air from outside and watch
how outside tries to hold on
to its air but it's no use against
the powerful man-made blades.

When you're old metaphors fly out
the window like a scrap of paper
you didn't know was important and
you're left with only whatever was
in your lap the day you were born,
which is whatever's left in front
of you now, you know, a little life
and a fan trying to keep you cool
against the heat.

Faith in gravity

Gradually I came to let go
of pretty much everything
I believed, belief that had
kept me warm at night—
and then up all night—
and to be honest scared me
that I had been
just riding on this hurling
blind world with no
flight plan. For a long time
my insecurity had seemed
preferable to staring the
universe in the face,
like lying and then lying
again and then trying to
cover it up with another lie;
it's hard work to keep track
of all that you accept
without getting caught
with your pants down.
So I gave up religion
because faith is such a
hard thing to believe in,
and then I gave up science
because faith is such a
hard thing to believe in.

Obituarians dream in happy words

The obituarian works
seven days a week not
because people are dying
but because they could be.
What I mean is he's on call.

The obituarian never takes
a lover because he has no way
to tell the truth; all he knows is
to tell every dead person they
were great and meaningful.
What I mean is he's lonely.

The obituarian has a way
with words. Those words can't
count a life, but they are
the living's only hope in death.
What I mean is he's a poet.

Home run

There is a name for when rich people can't decide
which of their houses to drive to for the holiday while
other people are discovering the nutritional value of
poverty, but I don't know what it is so I'm going to call it
Sometimes you're the baseball, sometimes you're the bat.

When I get to pick the teams, my designated hitter
will be the ball, which most of the time gets
the shit beat out of it, but every once in a while it
sails over the fence and the roar of the crowd erases
the pain as if the bruises weren't even there.

I wonder why we are all like onlookers in a sideshow,
believing that the snake oil will cure us, but we know
it's not true, but we still believe it is. We believe it
like we believe that when it's our turn to bat
the ball will rise up high, high above the cheap seats
and summer homes, and never come back.

Cub scout blows it with Catholic school girl

I'm sorry I didn't buy us tickets
for the dance. I had the money
sitting right there but I didn't know
how to talk to girls. Or dance.

I'm sorry I didn't stay in scouts
after the leader told me I had
to wear my uniform or else. God,
you looked good in your uniform.

I'm sorry I didn't make anything
of my life, sorry I didn't get that
degree, sorry I never memorized
the scouts' credo.

Except I'm not sorry, not sorry
I quit the scouts, not sorry I can't
spell catechism, not sorry
I had struggles.

I am sorry, though, that
I didn't buy those tickets.

The pursuit of happiness

I've been nothing but
potential my whole life,

holding my ticket to be
the next great writer,

too smart for school but
still aimed toward some

brick-walled college
just on potential's fumes.

Here I am now
with all that promise

stinking with the survival
groceries in the pantry,

remnants of
what could have, should have,

leaving me with this old man
shuffle and the knowing.

Nature/commerce

The fish in Rock Creek are UPS trucks
lined up to load out at the docks,

the blue jays are the teletype machines
from 1950s stock market movies,

the waving grass in the field down from
our house is the ocean on a warm day—

no—the piston driving any GMC engine,
and the dark and still of last night

are the union breaks we get so we can
go back out there and be more productive.

At the acupuncturist's

At the acupuncturist's I mention
something about my age and then
realize how silly that sounds, how I could
be that old, could be sixteen high school
careers, older than three people turning
the legal drinking age. It sounds like a joke
from the waiting room, like some 25-year-old
is trying to be funny by referring
to himself as an old man.

Some flightless dove followed me
around the yard yesterday. He had no place
left to go, because where can a dove go who
can't use the sky anymore? So I fed him
and for a second thought about what results
a rescue might bring for a pet dove, for instance,
if there might be acupuncture for birds

or something, but to retrieve him
might be more unbalanced than the cat
we both knew was waiting in the weeds.
I told myself this, that maybe the dove recognized
the objective nature of the world of death
more than I did and maybe he was okay with it all.

But right now I wish I knew an old legend,
from some culture I can't even pronounce,
that tells something about the dove turning
into a hawk, with new wings, and I wish it said
something about me telling a joke about my age,
or maybe even just a little hope to entertain us as
we're waiting for the acupuncturist,
waiting for the cat.

A handbook for water

If you want to know something about me
be prepared to ask this. Ask me this:
ask me about water.

If you want to know something about water
go find that place where Coyote Creek
bubbles up from some spring under King Mountain.
Find where it ran past me as a kid
through the pool that held my skipping stones
through the middle of my romping fields,
through the middle of my years.

Follow where it begins to call
itself the Rogue River
where it pushes and relents
and stumbles and cries against the rocks
until it is finally called this ocean,
where I am.
If you find that then, then
you will know something about water.

The first

The first day on the railroad I learned unlucky is just another word for laborer.

The first time I had sex was nine months before my son was born.

The first time I got divorced I figured out the things you can't believe could happen to you happen to you.

The first time I lost a child I already had the grief stored away.

The first sound I remember hearing was my mother's voice breathing a prayer for my wonderful life.

What we can't afford to tell second graders

There's some kid somewhere playing cello,
practicing the same three notes over and over
until his fingers ignite, but they tell him to keep
up his practice, and he does, and, of course,
he becomes very good and famous, etc.

As you might already suspect, this is the dream
we all have the night before we're called upon
to tell our classmates what we will be when
we grow up, signing contracts, touring the big
concert halls, our name announced on printed pages.

But when it's our turn in front of the class we hesitate,
remembering that the cello dream was the dream of
a dream, that our own dream was the one with sad
marriages and night shifts, first and last month's rent,
realization that the number of musicians in the world

is both fixed and secret, and old student cellos leaned up
in the backs of closets.

Anatomous

If you should rebuild me can you fill me up
out of a river and replace this slow blood
wandering around lost inside of me,
maybe looking for a heart,

install roll-down windows instead of eyes
that will watch instead of observe, squint
instead of judge and let in just a little
of that cool breeze I never see anyway

and maybe you have something to replace these
old hired hands I tried to give up to the bosses,
just like they tell you, sacrifice your hands
but keep the soul, but they wanted all my parts

and speaking of souls, have we decided if
they exist? I was going to ask for one
of those too, but it doesn't seem to go that
well with the world I've been wearing lately.

Helping a hard luck lady in her wheelchair to the county building

She asks if I'm embarrassed to be seen pushing her. When she gets tired and we stop we happen to be on the bridge and

I tell her to look at all the fish down there but she can't because of her diabetes, can't see them even though they're so thick there's barely room for water.

She tells me, hon, you're a pretty good guy but after she says people in the world aren't very nice anymore she upgrades me to really nice.

We stop at the mini mart to buy two diet Mountain Dews because they're on sale if you buy two and because she's diabetic, you know, no sugar.

The receptionist at the county barely looks up like I'm only one more in a long line of Samaritans looking for someone else to save.

And I say see you later, and she says next time I'll throw a couple of bucks your way and I walk on home past the fish still swimming upstream.

What if your job

I fooled myself for years that all the jobs
I worked were better than one long career
because without a career I had more time
to spend not thinking about work. But really,
like you, I'd rather not work at all. What if
we got paid for nothing, not even for doing
things we love to do, like the singer in a band,
where sure, it's fun but there's still pressure
to perform, but just for living. There would be
no ties between what you get paid and what
you do. You breathe, you get a check.

Once I got paid for how many pounds of beans
I picked. I could pick more beans than most of
the other workers but I wasn't any better, just faster
at picking beans. And anyway, all of us were
there just to get some money; who would pick
beans on an early summer morning if you
didn't have to? We stood in line for the weigher
to weigh our beans like we were waiting to get
picked for a playground team where you have to
wait until the very end just because you can't dribble
the ball, waiting in line to see what we were worth.

Thick as thieves

I wake up one morning
and there's no car in the
driveway but I'm not going to
call this theft; it's retribution,
paying me back for
my ancestry or maybe
for the time I stole
change from my father's
dresser or when I watched
the grocery checker accidentally
bag a free avocado and I
didn't say anything and I
took it home until it
burned a hole in my
counter and I had to
throw it away from guilt.

We are all thieves. We steal
air from each other,
compete for blades of
grass when we can't even
count all the ones we have,
burn our mouths on
free-trade coffee
and call it suffering
while bums outside wave
at the cold with cold hands
with no coffee, and we tell
our children to hammer
but steal their nails. The
car is gone but I'm not going
to call this theft.
I owe.

To the next dove that comes around here

What I missed was the science of the
angle the goshawk took to overcome
the dove in mid-flight, the critical
trajectory we sometimes mistake
for instinct, as if killing something
were in our blood, as if the vanquished
live under a cloud of destiny.

It must be instead something more
like the calculus at Los Alamos,
eight hours a day, five days a week,
year after year, to get all that math
just right, so that when the target
fills up your sight, all you have to do
is dive.

How God catches us cheating

Our roof mostly works, especially
on sunny days, but we still argue
about the leaks like we're charged
with apportioning a map with
new countries. Do you know
how many buckets you could
fill the attic with for the price
of one roof, I don't say out loud.

The mind is a funny thing.
It punishes the body, gives itself
a time-out for violations like coveting
or eating a grape without
paying for it and it can condemn
its master like a talk show host.

I don't fight fair. I hang the last roof-
we-didn't-need over her head like a judge
who's not sure what sentence to hand out
but then hear about it all night whispering
from a voice that sounds like mine
but without the dry rot.

Houses will decay whether or not the
roof leaks, and the rains will end up
inside of what will eventually become
outside, so what are a few drops of water
between friends?

Or so it seems to me

that when you see a duck standing
in front of the bank on your way
to buy beer, it's a sign. Not a sign
like when we pretend there's some
order in the world, or like there's
some list somewhere that compares
every move you make to what
move you should have made,

but a sign that this is not a normal
occurrence. It's not a sign that
it's going to be a bad day or that
you're going to get your beer half-off,
but a sign that the world doesn't
operate according to signs.

Still, when you see that duck you
have to pick it up and walk it clear down
to Rock Cove and set it down with the
other ducks and watch it fly straight out
over the river, as if there *were* some list
in the world, as if there *were* some order
and the duck is merely playing out its part.

But of course there is no order so you
pick up the duck just because it's a duck
on the sidewalk in the middle of town,
because you have to, because you
can't go back home empty-handed
without helping the world out
just a little. Or so it seems to me.

Natural selection poem

Every girl I loved
in high school or
at least every one
I dreamed about
ended up with
a boyfriend
from another school
and I hated them
for that because all
the chances I never
had anyway died again,
like running over
a dead animal on
your way home.
I know now they
were instinctively
driven to perpetuate,
to seek out their
best prospects,
the shiny athletes or
intellectual student
body presidents, so
their own babies would
defend the genome,
you know, date boys
from other schools.
I know now it was
just natural selection
because all of us wished
we carried that favored
gene too.

Building a legend out of Legos

My father repeated and added
to his stories so often they now have
lives of their own. Seriously, I think
some of them are naturalized citizens,
immigrating from foreign places like
old letters and often taking a seat
next to me in this kitchen, sometimes
late at night when I'm trying to sort out
other things

like why we so often want to write about
our fathers. My theory now is it's because
we want them to be godperfect—
I know, I know, too much psychology
but give me a second—maybe even *god* and,
having discovered the fallibility of a
god, we throw it back on the shoulders
of weak old men we can't forgive.

Tonight it's the story of the Marines versus
Korea, and last night the ascension from the
dirt-floor Arkansas story sat right there
where you're sitting and I laughed out loud
until I cried out loud when he said at my
father's California college they couldn't
understand Southerners when they talked.

The trophy case

The glass case just outside the gym doors
to me always meant loss, each space between
the trophies a defeat, all the games we didn't win.

I remember
the memorial picture of a girl, mixed in with
the golds and the silvers,

who had an argument with her mother
on the way to school one morning, opened
the car door, and jumped.

I suspect her place in the trophy case was to ease
her parents' pain, to let them know how much
the school understood by locking away their tragedy

inside clear glass with the most cherished of icons,
a dead girl next to the 1963 State Football Champions,
and by locking away the argument,

something so everyday but with the permanence
of an opposing team's winning touchdown,
and when that didn't work how her mother,

dangling in the moment, tried 7000 ways to fix
that morning, what she might have done differently,
maybe letting her daughter win the argument,

maybe driving another route,
maybe remembering to pick up that loaf of rye bread
on the way.

Life coaches

I've never been to a Tony Robbins'
revival, but I know how those
participants must feel. Once,
Tony came to me as my ex-wife.
She was inspirational at telling me
how to live my life better, to recognize
what the world wanted me to have,
how to be—here it comes—successful.
Sometimes I could even hear the
Robbins' cheerleaders cheering me on:
come on, they said in the background
of this poem, you can do it. All I had
to do was sign up for the program and
my successes would *have to* follow.

Except when you leave the packed
auditorium and it gets all quiet,
maybe late at night on your front porch,
maybe in a small town, and nobody's
there to cheer you on, even Tony,
who has left for another tour, then you
start to see that when you signed up
it's Tony who is getting successful
and you end up back at your day job,
alone, wondering what the hell
just happened.

The guy who couldn't see color

On some show this old guy cries for joy when he sees color for
the first time. Maybe seeing color is a desire we're born with,
I think, or maybe he already has an expectation of something
really special because he's been preached at his whole life about
how much he's been missing, like the kid who feels all left out

because the other kids got measles and he didn't, not that seeing
color is like getting measles, but maybe seeing only black and
white is something we'd choose, if we could, probably not. But
then, what has color ever done for us?

Nyel might not walk again. He got that black and white news
from a green hospital full of multi-colored machines,
not one of which will help him regain his apathetic white leg,
and I wonder if having two legs that work is a desire we're born
with, or is there a way one leg is better?

Poetry sometimes pushes the personal into the vast, revealing
a lesson we can sometimes agree with. Not here. I just want to tell
you about Nyel, how for so many years he loved to work, to run
his red bookstore, to cook colorful meals, to move his two good
legs.

I saw a pink skateboarder today on my way to a brown coffee
shop. He was moving down the sidewalk really good,
but he had no legs and a purple shirt and I have no way
to tell you how that has left me.

My life as money

I don't want you to think I only look at life
in terms of money but when I go to work on Monday
I'm a dollar sign, income for somebody else,
how much work can I do in how little time.

I come home and the house measures me
as square footage, the view from the deck
I don't have, how a second bathroom would help
the resale value, fix up the yellow lawn, etc.

When I'm in the store I watch people
watch me to see how much
I'm going to spend, to see
how big their bonuses will be.

Even love is money. Once someone
left me to go away to college to get a career
and there I was, holding hocked dreams
and working to make a square living.

I sit in the coffee shop
with a $3 coffee plus tip and wonder if
there's any other way to count a life
but there is no other way.

Mars

There was this show on the massive amount of food
prepared everyday on a luxury ship, thousands
of pounds of shrimp and chicken and unspeakable
numbers of workers trapped on that boat,
racing against the clock to make every meal perfect.
I don't even know if we have words to judge this.

Sometimes I don't feel like I belong here, like I'm
different in the way a shrimp is different
from a chicken, the way they look at
the world with either feathers or from
underneath the ocean and in the end sharing
space on someone's plate is all they have in common.

Sometimes I feel like I'm from another planet,
you know, like I'm lying there on someone else's plate.
Then I walk down the street watching everyone watch
themselves in store windows believing the same thing,
how different they are. And I start thinking, well, maybe
we are all from Mars or maybe we're already on Mars
and we've been here all along.

And if that's true, then maybe we're not so different after all.

Manifold destiny

Sixty years ago my parents moved out of L.A. to Oregon,
city to wild, leaving the smog they said, and they packed
with them all of the accoutrements of their tribe, alarm clocks,
metal tools, political songs and I'm guessing

the new neighbors looked at them suspiciously although
I can only assure you they never meant harm. And they absorbed
the country life fervently, bought pigs, milked cows,
just tried to fit in inside their worn city clothes.

I'm guessing this was also not looked upon favorably by the locals,
by whom I mean all those Californians who had come before them.
Look, I have no answer about whether my parents should have
immigrated into that small, tar-sided shack in the woods,

raised their own first-generation, borderless refugees
or stayed reclined under the heat of the California sun, but what
I can tell you is they've lived on that mountain for sixty years
and they act like they've been there forever.

Zero in the denominator

Until now I never understood math,
or at least the concept of zero in
the denominator. Teachers tried
to tell me that zero in the denominator
isn't nothing, or something, or anything;
it isn't even zero. They said instead it's a
question that can't be asked or answered,
like what would the world be like if someone
hadn't invented tires, or if you wouldn't
have left me standing so awkwardly on your
front porch so long ago now. Nobody
can answer what would have happened
so I spend my days not asking, and things
come and go and what might have been is not
something or nothing; it's a zero in the
denominator, just a wish whose candle
was never blown out.

Old maid

We all try to get what we can
out of life. Me, I could make do
if you give me a job that pays
enough to get me a good
restaurant meal once a month,
but no night shift.
I've had enough of that. Some
people would be content
just to have their kid back,
or to not have to fight some
other gang tonight.
Some people would be happy
to just hold on to their lives
for one more day.

There's this old maid I know
who says she will never get
married again, never wants
even a boyfriend around.
She's happy with her life
she says. And I say happy is
a day without being scared
someone is going to hit you—
hard—or not come home, or
come home and act like you're
not there. I say happy is a word
that can cover a lot of ground.

Multiple choice

Sometimes now I cry more
over the news, even knowing we
all have only a certain number
of tears, but other times I can't
bring myself to give one shit when
some hurricane lashes itself
against us or more people go missing
in this week's war, so I plan
to study to be a scientist so
I can reduce the news to one
big number because nobody
gets emotional over numbers,
or maybe a professor so I can
discuss the news in a lecture
and use it in a pop quiz
where the answer, "D. suffering,"
is always the right answer.

Crow spreads his wings

This Indian man is instructing us
about the ways of a native dance,
with illustrations and young people
regaled in their finest beaded clothing
and they sing and pound drums
and the dancers move in ways I have
never seen and the music is notes

I have never heard, like the sound
creek water makes hitting stones under
a distant crow. The man introduces
a new dance and he calls the dancer
by the wrong name and his young
daughter laughs at him just exactly
the way my daughter laughs at me.

A million crows fly over the world
and if we look up we will see a million
silhouettes, each one as different
as Gene Kelly is to these dancers,
but a daughter's laugh, that,
that sting of wrath wrapped inside
the music of a child's delight, I
think that's the same sound
no matter what dance you do,
no matter what creek you hear.

If I were to define religion

Say there's
an old friend someday
who mentions a name, mine,
or say there's a smell from
some small café or
even the hint of a spring day
like this one
out of the west,
holding off the
rest of winter.

Wherever you are
put down your fork.
Wrap the remaining bread
in a napkin and
walk back
here to this day.
Find it in yourself
to say "pleasant."
Wasn't it? Isn't it?

About the Author

Casey Killingsworth is a poet whose work has appeared in *The American Journal of Poetry*, *3rd Wednesday*, *Two Thirds North*, and other journals. His first book of poems, *A Handbook for Water*, was published by Cranberry Press in 1995, as well. He also has a book on the poetry of Langston Hughes, *The Black and Blue Collar Blues* (VDM, 2008). Casey has a degree from Reed College.